Original title:
Rising from Shadows

Author: Olivia Orav
ISBN HARDBACK: 978-9916-89-883-3
ISBN PAPERBACK: 978-9916-89-884-0
ISBN EBOOK: 978-9916-89-885-7

Wings unfurled from the Abyss

From depths of sorrow, rise anew,
A whisper calls, both pure and true.
With faith as light, we spread our wings,
Emerging strong from darkened things.

Embrace the dawn, let shadows flee,
In every heart, the spirit's key.
With every beat, a hymn is sung,
To praise the grace, forever young.

Beneath the Celestial Canopy

Beneath the stars, our hopes take flight,
In cosmic dance, a spark of light.
The heavens sing, a sacred song,
Uniting all, where we belong.

In silent prayers, our voices blend,
With trust that knows, the soul won't bend.
Each twinkle tells of love divine,
Beneath the sky, our spirits shine.

The Morning Star's Promise

The morning star, with gentle gleam,
Awakens hearts from darkest dream.
A promise made, in light's embrace,
To guide us through, with endless grace.

In tender rays, we find our way,
Each step in faith, a brand new day.
With hope ignited, fears dissolve,
In every soul, divine resolve.

In the Embrace of Mercy

In mercy's arms, we find our rest,
The weary souls, by love caressed.
Forgiveness flows, like rivers wide,
Binding the broken, side by side.

With every tear, a healing stream,
In grace we weave, our common dream.
In unity, we stand and call,
In mercy's heart, there’s room for all.

The Sacred Dance of Renewal

In the stillness of night,
Hearts awaken to grace.
Divine whispers ignite,
Souls lift in their space.

With each step we take,
A rhythm pure and free.
In the warmth of His love,
We dance in unity.

The earth bears our song,
As hope begins to rise.
In sacred connection,
We reach for the skies.

Let the shadows disperse,
In light we find the way.
Together we will sing,
At dawn of each day.

In the circle of trust,
We gather hand in hand.
In the dance of renewal,
We make our holy stand.

Reaching for the Eternal Light

In quiet moments we yearn,
For the glow of His grace.
With each prayer we return,
To seek His warm embrace.

The stars twinkle above,
A reflection of the soul.
Drawing closer in love,
We abandon the cold.

With faith as our guide,
We venture through the dark.
On paths where hope resides,
Each heart ignites a spark.

Together we will rise,
On wings of sacred peace.
In the heavens we gaze,
And find our hearts' release.

Reaching for the divine,
Through trials we are led.
In the light that shines bright,
Our spirits shall be fed.

Light Unveiled in the Gloom

When shadows dance around,
And fears begin to swell,
A flicker breaks the bound,
A soft and sacred spell.

In whispers of the dark,
The light begins to gleam.
With every tender spark,
We awaken from the dream.

Each heart holds a lantern,
A flame that will not cease.
In the depth, we discover,
The promise of His peace.

Through valleys of despair,
We walk with heads held high.
With hands outstretched in prayer,
We touch the endless sky.

In the gloom, we find warmth,
As love will draw us near.
Light unveiled will transform,
And banish every fear.

The Dawn of Redemption

As morning breaks anew,
Hope rises with the sun.
In grace, we are made true,
In Him, we're never done.

With each gentle whisper,
Forgiveness finds its way.
In love, the hearts grow crisper,
A promise for each day.

The past is washed away,
In streams of holy light.
We become what we say,
As we choose what is right.

In the warmth of His arms,
We shed our heavy chains.
The dawn brings new alarms,
Where joy forever reigns.

With every breath we take,
We celebrate the morn.
In union, hearts awake,
A new world shall be born.

Transcending Night's Embrace

In the shadows, hope does gleam,
Where souls awaken from their dream.
A dawn breaks, serene and bright,
Transcending all of darkest night.

With open hearts, we rise and pray,
In faith, we find the destined way.
Each step a whisper, soft and clear,
Guiding us through doubt and fear.

Beneath the stars, our spirits soar,
Embracing love forevermore.
Together, we shall find the light,
In unity, we transcend night.

Whispers of Celestial Ascent

In silence, wisdom finds its voice,
The heavens beckon, we rejoice.
Guided by the stars that shine,
We journey forth, the path divine.

Though trials rise, we do not fall,
For love transcends, it conquers all.
Each heartbeat echoes through the sky,
As dreams take flight, we learn to fly.

With every prayer, our souls entwine,
In whispered hopes, the light will shine.
The cosmos dances, pure and free,
In faith, we find our destiny.

The Breath of New Beginnings

With each dawn comes a fresh embrace,
A chance to grow, to seek His grace.
New beginnings rise each day,
As shadows fade, we find our way.

In quiet moments, hearts ignite,
The breath of dawn, a sacred light.
We cast away our chains of old,
In trust, our stories shall unfold.

The winds of change will softly blow,
In every heart, new seeds we sow.
With faith as guide, we step anew,
Embracing life as if brand new.

Illuminated by Faith

In realms of light, our spirits glow,
Illuminated by love's flow.
Each step we take, a sacred dance,
In faith, we find our true expanse.

When shadows loom and doubts appear,
We turn to love, cast off our fear.
In hands entwined, we stand as one,
Our journey bright beneath the sun.

With hearts ablaze, we rise and sing,
In joy, redemption we will bring.
Together, lifted by His grace,
As light shall guide us, face to face.

The Ascendant Prayer

In shadows deep, I seek Your light,
A whispered prayer in the night.
Lift my soul above the fray,
Guide my heart, Lord, on this way.

Each step I take, I feel Your grace,
A warm embrace in this vast space.
With every breath, I rise anew,
To find the path, Lord, leading to You.

Sanctify my weary heart,
From all the pain, I wish to part.
Your mercy flows like endless seas,
In faith, I trust; I seek my peace.

When burdens weigh and doubts draw near,
Your gentle voice, I long to hear.
O lift me higher, beyond despair,
In quiet moments, teach me prayer.

Through trials faced, I'll steadfast stand,
With open heart and lifted hand.
In love's embrace, my doubts subside,
In You, my Savior, I abide.

Echoes of Hope in Silence

In silence deep, the spirit sighs,
A whisper soft that never dies.
Hope lingers like the morning dew,
In heartbeats, Lord, I trust in You.

Your promises, like stars, so bright,
Illuminate the darkest night.
In quietude, my soul shall find,
The echoes of a love so kind.

Though shadows creep and fears invade,
In prayerful stillness, I am made.
Your presence calms the raging storm,
In arms of peace, my heart is warm.

With every breath, I seek the light,
Through darkened paths to reach the height.
The echoes call, I drift away,
In solitude, I come to pray.

Through trials faced, I rise once more,
Those echoes guide me to Your door.
In every silence, hope will sing,
The beauty of Your love is spring.

Illuminated by Faith's Flame

Amidst the night, a candle glows,
A beacon bright where darkness flows.
With faith as flame, my spirit soars,
Through trials faced, Your love restores.

Each flicker holds a promise true,
In joy and pain, my heart finds You.
Illuminate this weary path,
With every step, I feel Your wrath.

In gentle light, Your hand guides me,
To depths unknown, and yet I'm free.
To rise above, to walk in grace,
Illuminated by Your face.

As shadows dance and fears abound,
In faith's embrace, my hope is found.
I'll trust the flame to lead me home,
Through every step, I'm not alone.

In darkest hours, Your warmth I seek,
For in the silence, it's You I speak.
Illuminated by love's pure beam,
I walk in faith, I live the dream.

Ascension of the Weary

The weary soul finds rest in prayer,
Enfolded in Your tender care.
Through trials faced and burdens shared,
In seeking You, my spirit's paired.

With every step, the path unfolds,
A journey rich with stories told.
Ascend my heart, O Lord, I plea,
Embrace my soul, set my heart free.

In moments still, Your voice I hear,
A gentle whisper, calm and near.
The weight of doubt begins to lift,
In faith’s ascent, I find my gift.

Though storms may clash and shadows loom,
Your light will pierce the deepest gloom.
With heavy heart, I rise once more,
To meet the dawn, I'm called to soar.

In gravity of life’s despair,
I seek the heights, I breathe the air.
Ascension’s grace, I hold so dear,
In weary hearts, You draw us near.

From Shadows, New Paths Manifest

In the depths where darkness dwells,
A whisper calls, it softly knells.
Emerging light breaks through the veil,
From shadows comes a sacred trail.

With faith anew, we step ahead,
Each step a prayer, where hope is fed.
The road, though steep, shall guide our way,
For in our hearts, the truth will sway.

Through trials faced and burdens borne,
The spirit's breath, a soul reborn.
Transcending fears, our spirits rise,
Together reaching for the skies.

A vision clear, our purpose found,
In every heartbeat, love resounds.
With open hands, we dare to seek,
The light within, so strong, so meek.

The Illumination of Forgiven Souls

In the stillness, grace unfolds,
Casting warmth on weary folds.
Each heart, once heavy with regret,
In gentle light, all pain is met.

Whispers softly heal the past,
With tender hands, the spell is cast.
Forgiven wounds, the balm of time,
In love's embrace, we find our rhyme.

Shadows fade, the dawn appears,
Washing away the darkest fears.
We walk together, hand in hand,
In unity, our spirits stand.

Forgiveness, like a sacred balm,
Transforms the storm into a calm.
In every heartbeat, truth resounds,
With every breath, new grace abounds.

Hope’s Embrace in the Eclipse

In twilight's hush, the stillness grows,
A dance between the light and shadows.
Yet in this moment, hope ignites,
A beacon bright, through endless nights.

The world may darken, skies may weep,
Yet in our hearts, the promises keep.
Eclipsed not by despair or gloom,
But by the strength that flowers from bloom.

With every challenge, hope ascends,
In trials, we find where broken mends.
Through joy and pain, the spirit flies,
A testament to love that ties.

The light shall crest, the dawn shall break,
In unity, our spirits wake.
Through every shadow, we embrace,
A sacred bond, our chosen grace.

Shrouded Promises Delivering Light

In silence deep, the promise breathes,
With every whisper, the spirit weaves.
Though wrapped in clouds, the truth shall shine,
A radiant light, divinely timed.

Each hidden vow, each silent plea,
Resounds in echoes, setting free.
The heart, though shrouded, knows its way,
Through paths of trials, come what may.

In darkness held, our faith prevails,
A journey crafted in sacred tales.
With trust embraced, we seek the dawn,
The light shall rise, the night is gone.

Through every tear, a seed is sown,
In every struggle, love is grown.
With shrouded promises, we unite,
Delivering hope, creating light.

Flourishing in the Light of Truth

In dawn's embrace, we rise anew,
With hearts aglow, in faith we grew.
The Light of Truth, a guiding flame,
Illuminates our sacred name.

In whispers soft, the Spirit calls,
Through trials deep, our courage sprawls.
With every step, we bloom and thrive,
In Love's embrace, we come alive.

The path we walk may test the brave,
Yet in our souls, we find the wave.
A river pure flows from above,
With every breath, we sense His love.

The echoes of the holy sound,
In silence vast, His grace is found.
Beyond the veil, a promise lies,
In prayer's ascent, our spirits rise.

Together bound, we stand as one,
In unity, our victory won.
For in this light, we find our way,
To flourish bright, come what may.

Wings of Redemption

In shadows cast, we seek the light,
With humble hearts, we brave the night.
The flight of souls, through trials wide,
In faith, we soar, our hearts our guide.

Forgiveness blooms, a fragrant rose,
In every heart, compassion grows.
With wings of hope, we lift the weak,
In every word, the truth we speak.

The chains of sin, we cast aside,
In mercy's arms, we safely glide.
Each tear we shed, a seed we sow,
In grace, we find our path to grow.

The skies stretch wide, with open grace,
We seek the warmth, His sweet embrace.
In every struggle, find the strength,
For in His arms, we go the length.

So spread your wings, let courage reign,
In trials faced, through joy and pain.
For in the struggle, we will find,
The path to peace, our souls unbind.

The Path of the Enlightened

With every dawn, the spirit sings,
In wisdom's light, our journey brings.
The path we walk, with purpose clear,
In every step, the truth draws near.

Awake, arise, let love be known,
In every heart, a seed is sown.
Through valleys low and mountains high,
Our souls ascend, like birds we fly.

The wisdom of the ages speaks,
In gentle tones, it guides the meek.
With open hearts, we seek the way,
In every night, awaits the day.

Through trials faced, we stand in grace,
In silence deep, we find our place.
The path of light, forever bright,
In faith, we walk, towards the light.

Together bound, through joy and strife,
In every breath, the gift of life.
With open arms, embrace the day,
For in His love, the shadows fray.

Throughout the Trial, Hope Stirs

In sorrow's depths, the heart may ache,
Yet in the night, new dawn shall break.
Through trials fierce, our spirits stay,
In faith we rise, come what may.

The storm may roar, the winds may bite,
Yet in the dark, we seek the light.
With every tear, a prayer is born,
In every loss, a love reborn.

Through valleys low, we find our song,
In unity, we all belong.
For hope will stir, like dawn's first ray,
In every heart, it finds a way.

The strength we hold is not our own,
In silent trust, we're never alone.
With every rise, a lesson learned,
In every flame, our passion burned.

Together now, we face the trial,
With faith as guide, we find our smile.
For through the storm, we come to see,
In every struggle, we are free.

Ascending from the Abyss

In shadows deep, the spirit clings,
To whispered hopes, to fragile wings.
A flicker shines in the darkened night,
A call to rise, to seek the light.

Chains of despair, they start to break,
With every prayer, the heart awake.
The hand of grace extends its reach,
From depths of pain, a lesson's teach.

Silent cries, a journey's toll,
In faith we find a mended soul.
The narrow path begins to gleam,
In trials faced, we weave a dream.

Each step we take, toward the sky,
The sacred promise, we won't deny.
From ashes born, we stand anew,
In love's embrace, our spirits grew.

With every dawn, new hope is found,
As gratitude wraps us all around.
Ascending higher, our spirits soar,
In unity, we seek and explore.

Emergence of the Soul's Light

In quietude, the soul awaits,
A glimmer soft, it reverberates.
Through veils of doubt, a whisper grows,
The light within, it gently glows.

From barren fields, a flower blooms,
In winter's grip, the spirit grooms.
Awakening in sacred space,
The heart expands, it finds its grace.

In every tear, a story lies,
In every prayer, the spirit flies.
The journey long, yet sweetly bold,
With faith entwined, our truths unfold.

As night recedes, the dawn will rise,
A canvas brushed with golden skies.
The soul's light shines, a beacon bright,
Illuminating the path of right.

Together we reclaim our song,
In unity, we all belong.
Emerging strong, the light ignites,
In endless love, we face new heights.

Dawn's Embrace after Darkness

When shadows loom, and hope seems lost,
The sun will rise, despite the cost.
With every tear, we make a mark,
Dawn's embrace dispels the dark.

From fragile hearts, the courage springs,
In stillness, hear the promise sings.
The daybreak whispers, softly calls,
In faith, we rise when daylight falls.

The night may stretch, the fear may swell,
Yet in our hearts, the light will dwell.
Awakened spirits, hand in hand,
In love, we find a promised land.

Gentle breezes brush our cheeks,
As wisdom flows and softly speaks.
With every dawn, renewal comes,
In unity, the heart succumb.

With arms outstretched, we greet the morn,
In shadows past, we are reborn.
Dawn's embrace, our guiding light,
Together strong, we rise from night.

From the Depths to the Divine

In murky depths, the heart once wept,
But faith restored, it safely kept.
A journey long, through trials we tread,
From brokenness, our spirits fed.

In silence, echoes bloom anew,
With open hearts, we seek what's true.
The chalice filled, with love divine,
We lift our souls, from low to shine.

With every step, the shadows fade,
In light we walk, unafraid.
The path is lined with sacred grace,
In every heartbeat, we find our place.

From darkest night to radiant day,
In love's embrace, we find our way.
The depths transformed, our spirits soar,
In unity, we seek much more.

With gratitude, the song will swell,
In harmony, our hearts shall dwell.
From depths once lost, to heavens wide,
In peace and hope, we now abide.

The Radiance of the Undying

In shadows deep, a light appears,
Whispers of grace, drowning our fears.
The dawn unfolds, a sacred way,
Endless love guides us, come what may.

With every breath, the spirit flows,
A well of peace that gently glows.
In trials faced, we stand as one,
In faith's embrace, new life begun.

The stars above, a guiding hand,
In every heart, the promise stands.
Through storms of doubt, we seek the truth,
In every soul, the light of youth.

We gather here, the faithful choir,
United voices, soaring higher.
Each tear of joy, a prayer expressed,
In tender moments, we are blessed.

Thus let us walk on sacred ground,
In every silence, love is found.
With radiant hope, we shall ascend,
In the embrace of the Undying Friend.

Emblazoned by Consecrated Fire

In fervent hearts, a flame ignites,
A holy spark, through darkest nights.
With every prayer, the embers glow,
A warmth within, a truth to show.

Through trials faced, our spirits rise,
In every tear, a dream replies.
With passion bold, we found our place,
Embracing grace, we seek His face.

The sacred fire, consuming bright,
Illuminates our faith with light.
In sacred circles, we unite,
To share the warmth, to spread the light.

We stand as one, a faithful throng,
In harmony, we sing our song.
With hearts ablaze, we journey forth,
In love, we find our sacred worth.

Through trials keen, our spirits soar,
Emblazoned souls, forever more.
With every breath, the spirit's choir,
We rise anew, in consecrated fire.

The Sacred Rise of the Forsaken

In shadows cast, the least of these,
A calling heard upon the breeze.
With open arms, we share the grace,
A sacred rise in every place.

Through broken paths, we find our way,
With hearts attuned to love's display.
Each story told, a hushed refrain,
In unity, we heal the pain.

From ashes born, the spirit leaps,
In every soul, a promise keeps.
The light within cannot be quenched,
In faith alive, the bounds are drenched.

Together we rise, the meek and bold,
In every heart, the truth unfold.
A tapestry of lives entwined,
In love's embrace, our fate aligned.

Thus let us soar, all bruised and scarred,
In seeking truth, we stand unbarred.
With sacred hands, the world we mend,
The sacred rise, with love, we send.

Hearts Alight with Promise

In every heartbeat, grace bestowed,
A gentle breeze on life's long road.
With open eyes, we seek the dawn,
The dreams of hope, in us reborn.

Through trials faced, we join the fight,
With weary spirits, we claim the light.
In whispered prayers, a vow we share,
With faith renewed, we boldly dare.

The sacred garden, seeds we sow,
With loving hands, we guide their grow.
In every touch, a promise flows,
With hearts alight, our harvest grows.

The melody of peace resounds,
In every soul, a joy abounds.
With kindred spirits, we shall sing,
In every moment, blessings spring.

Thus let us rise, both meek and strong,
In every heartbeat, we belong.
With hearts aglow, we share the weight,
With promise bright, we stand as fate.

The Chariot of Deliverance

In shadows deep where hope may fade,
The chariot waits, a promise made.
With wings of light, it soars above,
Carrying hearts, embraced in love.

Through trials faced, the journey long,
In faith we rise, united strong.
Each tear we shed, a seed of grace,
In grace we find our destined place.

When burdens weigh and spirits bend,
The chariot rolls, our truest friend.
In whispered prayers, our voices blend,
With every call, our souls ascend.

Through valleys dark, through storms that rage,
The chariot moves, the turning page.
With every pulse, a heartbeat's call,
In love we trust, we won't let fall.

So ride with faith, let not fear reign,
For deliverance comes through the pain.
With hope ablaze, let spirits soar,
In the chariot's path, forevermore.

Lanterns Guided by the Divine

In twilight's glow, the lanterns shine,
Each flicker tells of love divine.
With gentle hands, they light the way,
In darkness deep, they softly play.

Through whispered winds, the prayers take flight,
In sacred trust, we seek the light.
Each flame a sign, a heart's desire,
As we are drawn, our souls inspire.

With every step, the lanterns beam,
Guided by faith, we dream the dream.
Together bound, we walk in truth,
In every moment, reclaim our youth.

Through valleys wide and mountains steep,
The lanterns burn, in vigil keep.
With gentle grace, they lead us on,
In the embrace of dawn's sweet song.

So raise your light, be bold and free,
Let every heart in love agree.
In unity, let shadows cease,
With lanterns bright, we find our peace.

The Sacred Heart from Depths

From depths unseen, the heart does swell,
In sacred pulse, our spirits dwell.
A bond unbroken, love's embrace,
A guiding star in time and space.

With every heartbeat, grace unfolds,
In whispered truths, the story's told.
Through trials faced and battles won,
The sacred heart will be our sun.

In quiet moments, visions clear,
The heart speaks softly, drawing near.
In darkest nights, it shines so bright,
A beacon drawn from love's pure light.

From storms we rise, as one we stand,
In sacred trust, united hand.
With each new dawn, renewal comes,
Awakening hope, the past succumbs.

So cherish deep the sacred heart,
In every breath, let love impart.
Through time and space, it leads the way,
In harmony, forever stay.

Celestial Paths Through the Night

Beneath the stars, our spirits soar,
On celestial paths, forevermore.
With every twinkle, a love profound,
In the night sky, our hopes are found.

The moonlight dances, whispers sweet,
Guiding our steps, as shadows greet.
Through cosmic trails, our souls align,
In universal love, we're entwined.

With every star, a promise shines,
In sacred whispers, hearts confine.
Through depths of night, the journey calls,
In unity's grace, we break down walls.

As constellations weave their tale,
In sacred strength, we shall prevail.
With faith as our sail, we venture wide,
Through celestial paths, we will abide.

So raise your voice to the heavens high,
Let every heart in wonder sigh.
For through the night, the stars will guide,
In love's embrace, we shall reside.

Veils of Illusion Torn Apart

In shadows deep, where doubts reside,
The truth shines forth, a faithful guide.
Through veils of night, our spirits soar,
Awakening love, forevermore.

Beneath the stars, where whispers blend,
Our hearts unite, the soul's true friend.
In clarity, we seek the light,
Illusions fade in Heaven's sight.

With every prayer, the silence breaks,
In sacred space, our spirit wakes.
We cast away the chains of fear,
In unity, the path is clear.

Transcending doubts, we rise above,
Embracing grace, eternal love.
In harmony, the world transforms,
As beauty blooms in countless forms.

So let us walk, the journey vast,
With open hearts, the die is cast.
In faith, we find our sacred art,
As veils of illusion torn apart.

The Choir of the Silent Heart

In stillness deep, the spirit sings,
A whisper soft, of sacred things.
Together we, in silence dwell,
A choir blessed, where love can swell.

With every breath, we harmonize,
In reverence, our souls arise.
No need for words, just hearts laid bare,
In silent grace, we're free from care.

Resonance found in gentle peace,
The burdens lift, our worries cease.
In shared reflection, we draw near,
The melody of hope is clear.

Beyond the noise, the world may bring,
We find our strength in quieting.
The pulse of life, a sacred part,
Within the choir of the silent heart.

Together bound, we face the day,
With open hearts, we find our way.
In unison, let voices blend,
The sacred song, a love to send.

Ascending the Temple Steps

Each step we take, a journey grand,
To sacred heights, we lend our hand.
In faith we rise, our spirits bloom,
With every breath, we chase the gloom.

Draped in light, our hearts ignite,
Through trials faced, we seek the right.
The temple stands, with wisdom vast,
A beacon bright, a guide steadfast.

Through darkened paths, our courage grows,
With every tear, the spirit shows.
In unity, we lift our eyes,
To meet the dawn, to touch the skies.

Trust in the climb, let fear depart,
With every step, a brand new start.
Together bound, we face the quest,
Ascending high, we find our rest.

In joy we sing, as love unfolds,
In sacred halls, our truth beholds.
With hearts aligned, we shall not weep,
For at the summit, joy runs deep.

The Sacred Dance of Renewal

In twirling grace, the spirits flow,
A dance of love, the truth we know.
In circles wide, our hearts align,
With every beat, a spark divine.

As seasons change, the rhythms shift,
In sacred moves, we find our gift.
With every turn, our souls set free,
In the dance of life, we find decree.

With laughter bright, we shed our past,
In joy, we learn that love will last.
Within this space, we're not alone,
In unity, our spirits hone.

So let us sway, with passion's might,
Through shadows cast, we seek the light.
The sacred dance, our hearts renew,
With every step, we're born anew.

In harmony, our spirits rise,
With open hearts, we touch the skies.
As dancers weave through time and space,
The sacred dance, a pure embrace.

Shining Through the Ruins

In shadows deep, where hopes lay bare,
A whisper stirs, a gentle prayer.
The cracks do glow, the light breaks free,
Emerging faith, a steadfast plea.

Through broken walls and faded dreams,
The light descends in golden beams.
In every heart, a spark ignites,
Rekindling love and endless sights.

Though storms may rage, and winds may howl,
The strength within begins to prowl.
With every step, we rise once more,
Together, find what we implore.

In ruins high, our spirits soar,
Through darkest nights we seek the shore.
With hands entwined, we walk the way,
For light shall lead, and darkness fray.

A testament of grace and fight,
In every soul, the dawn's pure light.
We gather strength from all that's past,
In faith, we stand, steadfast and fast.

The Light Beyond Sorrow's Veil

In tears we shed, a sacred stream,
Each drop holds hope, each sigh a dream.
The veil of sorrow, thin and frail,
Hides a promise that will prevail.

Through valleys dark, the shadows creep,
Yet still our hearts, in silence, keep.
A beacon shines, though far away,
It calls us forth, to brighter day.

When burdens weigh and spirits tire,
Lift up your gaze, ignite the fire.
For faith, like dawn, shatters the night,
Revealing paths, illuminating light.

In every loss, a lesson learned,
From ashes rise, our hearts still burned.
The strength of love shall always clutch,
With gentle hands, it heals so much.

Beyond the veil, the promise stands,
In every heart, divine commands.
We weave our sorrows into grace,
In love's embrace, we find our place.

Rising Waters of Compassion

In stillest depths, where silence dwells,
Compassion flows, like gentle bells.
The rising tides of mercy rise,
Embracing hearts, with no disguise.

Each tear released, a pulse of grace,
We find our strength in love's warm embrace.
When pain surrounds, and hope seems lost,
Together we rise, no matter the cost.

The waters swell, purifying streams,
A river of kindness, woven dreams.
In unity's bond, we take our stand,
With open hearts, we understand.

To hold another in gentle care,
Is to touch the heavens, breathe the air.
Compassion’s gifts will light the way,
Guiding us forth, come what may.

From depths of sorrow, joy shall ignite,
Together we sail, through darkest night.
With rising waters, we shall mend,
A tapestry of love, without end.

Stones of Struggle, Blossoms of Grace

Upon the path, the stones do lie,
Each one a tale, a joyful sigh.
With every step, we feel their weight,
Yet in the struggle, we find our fate.

For from the earth, the flowers bloom,
In cracks of stone, dispelling gloom.
A testament to strength and care,
In every heart, a will to share.

The struggle shapes, the spirit grows,
In gardens tended, grace bestows.
From trials faced, resilience shines,
With every petal, hope entwines.

So gather stones, each burden bare,
Transform them into beauty rare.
For through the pain, the lessons trace,
A life embraced, in full of grace.

Let not the weight of sorrow bend,
For on this journey, we shall mend.
With every step, we rise and face,
The stones of struggle, blossoms of grace.

Light on the Path of the Faithful

In shadows deep, the heart will yearn,
A guiding hand, for truth we learn.
Each step we take, a prayer ascends,
In faith we trust, our soul transcends.

The dawn breaks forth, with promise bright,
Illuminating the way of light.
Through trials faced, we find our strength,
With love divine, we go the length.

In silence keen, the whispers call,
To walk with grace, we will not fall.
With every breath, a hymn we sing,
In harmony, our spirits cling.

With spirits bold, we rise and soar,
Upon the winds, we seek for more.
For in the light, our path is clear,
We tread with faith, and banish fear.

So let us journey, hand in hand,
In unity, we take a stand.
For every heart, a shining flame,
Together we extend His name.

The Resilient Heart's Pilgrimage

Through valleys low, and mountains high,
Our hearts will beat, and never die.
With every step, we face the strife,
In trials tough, we find our life.

Each burden borne, a cross to share,
A testament of love and care.
With every tear, a lesson learned,
In every heart, a fire burned.

With hope as our unyielding guide,
We walk the path, with arms spread wide.
Through storms that rage, we will not sway,
In faith, we find the light of day.

The road is long, yet we will stand,
In every footfall, a steady hand.
For in our souls, the truth we hold,
A story of the brave and bold.

And when we reach the journey's end,
In every heart, a life we'll mend.
For every wound, a faith renewed,
A resilient heart, forever true.

Rebirth through Divine Mercy

From ashes rise, a heart reborn,
In mercy's light, we find our dawn.
With every breath, a second chance,
In love's embrace, we learn to dance.

The past may haunt, but grace will reign,
A cleansing touch, to soothe our pain.
In every sin, forgiveness flows,
In tender hearts, His mercy glows.

As petals bloom from winter's freeze,
Our spirits lift, in gentle breeze.
Through trials faced, His love sustains,
Rebirth in Him, brings sweet refrains.

In every tear, a seed is sown,
In fertile ground, our faith has grown.
For in His hands, our lives align,
In mercy's warmth, our souls entwine.

So let us stand, in light adorned,
With grateful hearts, forever warmed.
For in His grace, we rise anew,
A testament of love so true.

Wings of Grace Unfurled

Above the clouds, our spirits soar,
On wings of grace, forevermore.
With hearts aflame and souls alight,
In faith we trust, through darkest night.

Through trials fierce, we lift our eyes,
In every heart, the spirit flies.
With courage sewn, our lives unite,
Together strong, we spread the light.

In sacred whispers, hope resounds,
A melody of love surrounds.
With open arms, we greet the dawn,
In every step, His path we're on.

So let us rise, with voices clear,
In harmony, we quell all fear.
For in the grace that freely flows,
Our spirit's strength forever grows.

With every thought, our prayers ascend,
To touch the hearts that need a friend.
For in this journey, love prevails,
With wings of grace, our hope unveils.

The Sacred Flame Rekindled

In the stillness of the night,
A spark begins to glow,
Hearts gather round the light,
In unity we grow.

From the ashes of despair,
We rise, our spirits soar,
With faith beyond compare,
We seek what lies in store.

Oh, the warmth of sacred fire,
Awakens dreams anew,
Each breath, a sweet desire,
To walk with Him, so true.

Let the embers dance and sway,
In rhythm with the breeze,
We embrace the dawning day,
With hearts at perfect ease.

Through trials we shall endure,
With love, the flame will last,
In Him, we find our cure,
The future, bright and vast.

Melodies of the Redeemed

In the silence, hear the sound,
Of voices raised in prayer,
Melodies of joy abound,
A symphony we share.

Each note, a story told,
Of grace that sets us free,
A harmony of hearts bold,
In perfect unity.

Together we shall sing,
With courage in our souls,
To the heavens, let us bring,
Our triumphs and our goals.

From the depths of sorrow's night,
We rise with pure delight,
In shadows, we find light,
As faith takes gentle flight.

With every breath we take,
Let praises fill the air,
In love, we do awake,
To blessings everywhere.

A Pilgrimage from Shadows

Journey forth through winding roads,
With faith to guide the way,
Each step lightens our loads,
As dawn ignites the day.

In the valley, hope resides,
Where angels sing in grace,
With each prayer, our hearts abide,
In the sacred space.

Through thickets of despair,
We tread with whispered dreams,
Knowing love awaits us there,
Beyond the shadowed seams.

In the distance, light draws near,
A beacon shining bright,
We shed our every fear,
In pursuit of the light.

With each mile we traverse,
Our spirits set to soar,
In this pilgrimage, we rehearse,
The peace we seek and more.

Celestial Conversations

In the silence of the night,
We listen to the stars,
Whispers float on gentle light,
As if they bear our scars.

Each twinkle tells a tale,
Of love that knows no end,
Hearts entwined, we shall not fail,
In faith, we find our friend.

Beneath this vast expanse,
We ponder life's great design,
In every glance, a chance,
To glimpse the divine.

With every prayer we send,
To the heavens up above,
We find solace, we transcend,
In grace, we're wrapped in love.

Together, we unite,
In this celestial dance,
Creating joy and light,
With every sacred chance.

Transformation in the Divine Embrace

In the stillness of the night,
Hearts awaken, seeking light.
A whisper calls from beyond,
In His love, we are reborn.

Chains of doubt begin to break,
As we yield to the path we take.
In surrender, we find grace,
Lost souls mended in His embrace.

Mountains crumble, fears take flight,
Fingers grasping Heaven's height.
From the ashes, hope will rise,
In His arms, the spirit flies.

Every shadow turned to gold,
Stories of the meek unfold.
In the silence, we are one,
Transformed by grace, by His own Son.

Each moment blooms, a sacred dance,
In His presence, we advance.
With faith unshaken, hearts aligned,
Together we awaken, souls entwined.

The Light’s Gentle Persistence

In the dawn of every day,
Light breaks forth to guide our way.
Gentle beams through window panes,
Whispers hope through life's refrains.

Clouds may loom, yet cannot stay,
The sun will find its path today.
Darkness trembles at His call,
In His warmth, we rise, not fall.

Through valleys deep, and shadows cast,
His light persists, it holds us fast.
In every heart, a flicker glows,
A flame of love that never goes.

Moments fleeting, yet so divine,
In the stillness, we entwine.
Each heartbeat sings a sacred song,
In His presence, we belong.

Stars above, a radiant guide,
In His brilliance, we abide.
Each step forward, a step of grace,
In the light's embrace, we find our place.

Streams of Water from Stone

In barren lands, hope's sweet refrain,
Life emerges, breaking chains.
From the rock, pure waters flow,
Refreshment found where none could grow.

With every thirst, a promise flows,
A tender heart, the Spirit knows.
In drought and struggle, faith will rise,
Quenching souls, where mercy lies.

Wounds of earth, yet grace remains,
In the desert, love sustains.
From parched souls, redemption springs,
In His hands, the healing brings.

Flowing rivers, deep and wide,
In His name, we will abide.
With every drop, a life reborn,
Streams of joy from hearts once worn.

As life unfolds, we drink anew,
His blessings pour, a faithful view.
In every flow, a journey dear,
Streams from stone, His promise clear.

Celestial Eyes Beholding Change

In the vastness of the night,
Stars look down, a guiding light.
Celestial eyes that see the heart,
In their gaze, we play our part.

Transformations whisper sweet,
In shadows, dark, and trials meet.
Each moment captured, sacred space,
In the sky, our dreams embrace.

Change is woven through our days,
Yet in His love, we seek our ways.
With every shift, His hands will mold,
New beginnings, tales of old.

Through storms that wash our tears away,
Celestial eyes, they bid us stay.
In their glow, we shed the past,
In their warmth, our futures cast.

Guided by the stars above,
In their constellations, we find love.
With every change, we rise anew,
In His light, our vision true.

From Gloom to Celestial Radiance

In shadows deep, hope starts to rise,
Faith emerges, beneath the skies.
From trials faced, we gain our light,
A beacon bright, dispelling night.

With whispered prayers that softly soar,
Hearts uplifted, forevermore.
In trembling hands, we seek His grace,
Transforming darkness, revealing His face.

Each step we take, the path unfolds,
A journey rich, with stories told.
From sorrow's grip, we find release,
In reverent peace, our spirits cease.

Celestial radiance warms the soul,
Mending fractures, making whole.
In sacred circles, joined in love,
We rise as one, to heights above.

With every tear, new growth shall spring,
In faith's embrace, our hearts take wing.
From gloom we rise, eternally free,
In His embrace, we find to be.

The Covenant of Second Chance

Through trials faced, our spirits break,
Yet in the dark, new paths we take.
Grace abounds in every stride,
Together, we shall turn the tide.

A second chance, a gentle call,
Forgiveness blooms, we rise, not fall.
His promise etched upon our hearts,
In every end, a new life starts.

With outstretched hands, He guides us near,
In every whisper, conquering fear.
Through storms of doubt, we find our way,
In sacred light, we choose to stay.

The covenant forged in love divine,
With each new dawn, our spirits shine.
We gather strength from all who pray,
In unity, we find our way.

From ashes rise, renewed in trust,
Transformed by love, we must, we must.
In every break, a chance to mend,
In His embrace, our hearts transcend.

Spirit's Pathway to the Sun

In quiet woods, where whispers dwell,
The spirit beckons, hear its swell.
With every breath, we find our path,
In nature's grace, we feel love’s wrath.

The sun, a guide, in skies so wide,
Illuminates where hearts confide.
Each step we take, the journey grows,
A sacred bond that ever flows.

Through winding trails, with trust we roam,
Finding solace, we feel at home.
The spirit’s voice, both fierce and soft,
Calls us higher, to soar aloft.

In moments still, we find the way,
As shadows dance, we greet the day.
With open hearts, the sun’s embrace,
Leads us onward, to sacred space.

By spirit’s hand, the truth unfolds,
In every heart, a story holds.
From dark to light, our souls shall run,
In light we find, our path begun.

Embracing the Celestial Dawn

Awake, O soul, at dawn's first light,
With gentle hands, let love take flight.
In blooming fields, the colors shift,
A promise born, the greatest gift.

The celestial dawn paints skies anew,
With each soft hue, our hearts renew.
In unity, we rise and sing,
To greet the hope that morning brings.

In sacred stillness, we reflect,
On journeys bold, and paths we'll trek.
With open arms, we claim our space,
Embracing love, in endless grace.

With every heartbeat, spirits weave,
In bonds of trust, we dare believe.
Through trials faced, we stand as one,
In harmony, our hearts have spun.

So let us dance beneath the skies,
Embracing dawn, where spirit flies.
In sacred moments, together drawn,
We celebrate the celestial dawn.

The Ascension of Faith's Whisper

In quietude of night, it starts to rise,
A whisper soft, beneath the starry skies.
It beckons hearts from shadows deep,
To trust in light, and in faith, to leap.

The dawn it brings, a promise clear,
To mend the broken, to cast out fear.
With gentle hands, it lifts the soul,
Restoring hope, making the spirit whole.

Each prayer, a thread, in tapestry spun,
Woven with love, binding everyone.
In unity, we strive and stand,
Guided by faith, led by His hand.

Upon the hills, the echoes sound,
Of ancient truths, in silence found.
Through valleys low, our voices rise,
In harmony beneath the skies.

So let us soar, on wings of grace,
Embracing light, in faith we place.
For in the night, a whisper gleams,
In hearts aflame, fulfilling dreams.

The Glorious Revelation of Dawn

When night departs and shadows flee,
A light emerges, bold and free.
It breaks the chains of dark despair,
Revealing love, beyond compare.

With hues of gold, the day is born,
A sacred hope, where souls are worn.
In every heart, the spark ignites,
A glorious truth awakens sights.

From morning's kiss, the earth will sing,
Of grace renewed, and joy we bring.
Each song a prayer, each step a vow,
To walk in light, here and now.

As sun ascends, the shadows fade,
Divine embrace, in love displayed.
The world aglow, a sacred trust,
In faith we gather, in hope we must.

So lift your gaze, to skies so bright,
Embrace the dawn, the gift of light.
For in this moment, life is found,
A glorious revelation, all around.

Breathing Life into the Forgotten

In silent halls of memory's keep,
Lie dreams abandoned, hopes unsweeped.
With tender grace, a breath is shared,
Awakening hearts, with love declared.

The weary souls, once lost in night,
Now rise anew, reclaimed by light.
Each whisper soft, a gentle call,
To all who wandered, to rise, not fall.

From ashes deep, new life will bloom,
In every heart, dispelling gloom.
With every tear, a chance to see,
The beauty in each destiny.

The lost are found, the broken mend,
In love's embrace, we learn to bend.
To breathe anew, in strength restored,
Reclaiming all, with one accord.

As light cascades, over land and sea,
Reviving dreams, setting spirits free.
No longer dwells that sense of strife,
Breathing life into the forgotten life.

The Shepherd’s Call in Twilight

When twilight falls, and stars appear,
The Shepherd's voice, we'll always hear.
In shadows cast, a gentle guide,
With love and grace, He'll walk beside.

Through fields of gold and valleys wide,
He leads us forth, with heart and stride.
In every whisper, comfort flows,
In every trial, His spirit knows.

A soft refrain, in evening’s breeze,
He calls us close, assuring ease.
In darkest times, He lights the way,
With hope renewed, come what may.

As stars align and night unfolds,
The stories of His love retold.
In quiet moments, He speaks our name,
In every heart, igniting flame.

So follow forth, through night and day,
With trust in Him, we’ll find our way.
For in our hearts, the Shepherds dwell,
In twilight’s glow, all will be well.

Hope’s Resurrection

In the valley of despair, light breaks,
Hope blossoms forth, like morning's dew.
Faith rises gently, banishing fears,
With every heartbeat, love renews.

From ashes of sorrow, joy is born,
A spirit reborn, in grace we stand.
Hands raised in gratitude, hearts adorn,
A path illuminated, brightly planned.

Whispers of solace, angels close,
Each trial met with divine embrace.
Strength within us, tenderly grows,
In unity's call, we find our place.

As the sun sets upon the night,
Shadows retreat, revealing the way.
In darkest moments, trust the light,
For in our hearts, hope's flames will stay.

Through storms we sail, on faith we ride,
Together we rise, a living creed.
With every dawn, love as our guide,
In hope’s resurrection, we are freed.

The Divine Whisper of Dawn

The first light stirs, a sacred sound,
A gentle breeze, soft and divine.
When night surrenders, grace is found,
The world awakens, hearts align.

Each golden ray a promise clear,
Revealing paths we're meant to tread.
In silence, listen, the truth draws near,
The whispering dawn, where dreams are fed.

Birdsong dances in the morning air,
Creation breathes anew, so bright.
With every heartbeat, love declares,
A symphony of hope ignites the night.

The sky unfolds in colors bold,
Heaven's canvas paints our day.
In this embrace, let souls behold,
The divine whisper guiding our way.

As shadows lift, we find our prayer,
In each moment, grace does flow.
Together we rise, light in the air,
In dawn's embrace, our spirits glow.

Enlightenment through Shadows

Beneath the stars, darkness resides,
In shadows deep, truth often hides.
Yet through the veil, glimmers ignite,
Illuminating hearts with sacred light.

Lessons learned in toil and strife,
Through pain and struggle, we gain sight.
With each trial, a wisdom grows,
In quiet moments, the spirit knows.

The moon's soft glow, a guiding friend,
Transforms the night from foe to mend.
In solitude found, we seek and find,
The light within, a divine design.

With open hearts, we face the night,
Embracing shadows, we seek the light.
In every corner, grace bestowed,
Enlightenment blooms on life’s long road.

As darkness fades, our fears release,
In unity’s bond, we find our peace.
Through shadows’ dance, we learn to rise,
In every heartbeat, the spirit flies.

Awakening to Celestial Promises

In the stillness of the morn, we rise,
Awakening hearts to the sky's embrace.
Celestial promises, whispered sighs,
Guide us gently in this sacred space.

Each star a beacon, shining bright,
Reminding souls of love's devotion.
In unity's call, we find our light,
Eternal grace, boundless as the ocean.

Nature's hymn, a sacred song,
Harmonizing with the pulse of time.
In every moment, we belong,
To the symphony of the divine.

With open arms, the heavens sing,
Inviting all to come and see.
As we awaken, hope takes wing,
In celestial promises, we are free.

The sun ascends, dispelling fears,
A tapestry of light unfolds.
In faith and love, we dry our tears,
Awakening joy, our story told.

The Clarity Beyond the Veil

In the stillness, whispers rise,
Truth unveiled before our eyes.
Heaven's light breaks shadows wide,
Guiding souls, our hearts confide.

Years of longing fade away,
In His presence, night turns day.
Faith ignites, a flame so bright,
Leading us through darkest night.

Angels sing in harmonies sweet,
Gathered as the faithful meet.
With each prayer, a bond we weave,
In His love, we shall believe.

Journeying through trials and tears,
Finding hope that calms our fears.
In the stillness, we will wait,
'Til the dawn of heaven's gate.

When we reach that sacred shore,
In His peace, we'll need no more.
All is clear and all is whole,
In the clarity of our soul.

In the Embrace of Grace

Tender whispers in the night,
Grace enfolds, a gentle light.
With each breath, a sacred song,
Inviting all to join the throng.

Hearts uplifted, spirits soar,
In His love, we seek no more.
Every burden fades away,
In His embrace, we find our way.

Mercy flows like rivers wide,
Washing over, setting aside.
Chains of doubt are gently broken,
In this moment, love's unspoken.

Through the storm, we stand as one,
Witnessing the rising sun.
Every shadow bids farewell,
In His grace, we rise and dwell.

Together walking hand in hand,
In His presence, we will stand.
Trusting, hoping, loving still,
In the embrace of His great will.

The Resplendent Offering

From our hearts, we give our all,
In His name, we heed the call.
Every gift, a sacred trust,
Sown in love, adorned with lust.

Bread and wine, a feast divine,
We unite, our spirits shine.
Joining voices, hearts ablaze,
In the light, we sing His praise.

Time and talent, all we share,
In our tasks, His love laid bare.
Every act a precious seed,
Harvested by the hands in need.

As we toil, we find our grace,
In unity, His warm embrace.
Let our offerings be a song,
Of love unending, pure, and strong.

With grateful hearts, we lift our hands,
Breathing life to His commands.
In this moment, all is well,
In the resplendence, we shall dwell.

Herald of the New Morning

With the dawn, a promise new,
Hope awakens, bright and true.
Every shadow fades away,
In His light, we find our way.

Birds are singing, skies unfold,
Stories of His love retold.
Each sunrise, a gift from above,
An invitation to His love.

Hands held high, we celebrate,
Life renewed, we contemplate.
Grace abounding, joy we find,
In the beauty, hearts aligned.

Mountains bow, and rivers flow,
In His presence, peace we sow.
New beginnings, endless grace,
Herald of the new morning's face.

Every heartbeat sings His praise,
In our lives, His light we raise.
With each day, a chance to grow,
In the love that we bestow.

So let us walk, hand in hand,
Toward the promise of the land.
Heralds of a morning bright,
In His love, we find our light.

Breaking Chains, Finding Wings

In shadows deep, the heart cries out,
Chains of despair surround the soul.
Yet faith ignites, a flickering flame,
Breaking the bonds, we become whole.

With every step, we rise and soar,
The weight of doubt falls far behind.
In grace we trust, our spirits free,
Finding the strength in love aligned.

Each trial faced, a lesson learnt,
Divine light guides us on our way.
Through darkest nights, we seek the dawn,
In silence, hear the angels say.

Hope like a dove, it lifts and glides,
Carving a path through the storm's wrath.
With every struggle, we gain our wings,
In unity, we walk the blessed path.

Let faith be our shield in this life,
As we embrace the skies above.
In God's great plan, we stand as one,
Breaking the chains, we find our love.

Awakening the Spirit's Lament

In quiet hours, the spirit sighs,
A whisper lost in time's embrace.
Awake, O heart, to sacred truth,
In each lament, we seek His grace.

The journey long, through valleys low,
Where shadows dance with heavy hands.
Yet hope arises like the sun,
In faith we trust, as Heaven plans.

With every tear, a prayer ascends,
Towards the skies where promise shines.
In sorrow's depths, we find our voice,
An echo of the Divine designs.

Embrace the pain, it shapes the soul,
Each wound a step towards the light.
The spirit’s cry, a sacred call,
Through darkness comes the dawn's delight.

Awakening now, the heart beats pure,
In unity, we rise again.
From loss, the spirit finds its song,
A melody of love, not pain.

Doves Amongst the Thorns

In gardens wild where thorns reside,
Doves take flight, embodying peace.
With gentle wings, they lift our hearts,
In trials fierce, our fears release.

Beneath the weight of whispered woes,
The dove alights, so soft, so near.
A symbol of the promise made,
In each embrace, we shed our fear.

The thorns that prick may teach us well,
To find our strength in love’s pure light.
For in each struggle, blossoms bloom,
The spirit soars, embracing flight.

With every tear, the petals fall,
Yet hope replenishes the ground.
In unity, we find the grace,
In fragile beauty, love is found.

So let the doves, in silence, sing,
A song of joy amidst the thorns.
For peace can thrive with love's embrace,
In every heart, a new dawn forms.

The Seraphim’s Soothing Whisper

In celestial realms, the angels glide,
Seraphim's wings, a gentle breeze.
They sing of hope, of love divine,
In the stillness, hearts find peace.

Their whispers drift through heavens wide,
A symphony of grace bestowed.
In every soul, they light the spark,
Guiding the lost along the road.

With tender touch, they heal the scars,
Transforming pain to sacred grace.
In night’s embrace, their warmth surrounds,
Assuring us, we’re not misplaced.

The light they bear ignites the dark,
A beacon bright amid the strife.
When burdens weigh, their voices rise,
Reminding us of eternal life.

So let the seraphs guide our way,
In every trial, their love shall shine.
With soothing whispers in our hearts,
We dance in faith, forever aligned.

Enkindled by the Divine Touch

In silence, whispers of grace flow,
Hearts alight, where love's embers glow.
Each breath speaks truth, divinely spun,
Awakening souls, one by one.

In prayer's embrace, spirits arise,
Seeking strength beneath vast skies.
Fingers entwined in hope's warm clutch,
Together we rise, enkindled by touch.

Through trials faced, faith will ignite,
A compass guiding in darkest night.
In every tear, a lesson learned,
From ashes of loss, our hearts discerned.

The sacred pulse of life we hear,
In every heartbeat, the Divine near.
With outstretched arms, we reach above,
Cradled in infinite, boundless love.

So let us walk this holy road,
With each step, lift the heavy load.
In kindness shared, our spirits touch,
In unity found, we flourish so much.

The Hidden Beacon's Call

In shadows deep, a voice does sing,
Guiding lost souls, hope's gentle wing.
The beacon's glow, though faintly cast,
Draws weary hearts to peace at last.

Through tempest's roar and night so vast,
The Light reveals paths to the past.
In the silence, truth does unfold,
A story of love, eternally bold.

In secrets kept by time's cruel hold,
Wisdom whispers, a promise told.
Every flicker, a spark divine,
Leading us to the sacred line.

Hearts entwined in prayer and grace,
Finding solace in this space.
For in the dark, we grasp the dawn,
And with each step, our fears are gone.

The hidden call, now loud and clear,
Unites our spirits, draws us near.
A journey blessed by love's embrace,
As we wander home, to sacred place.

In the Refuge of Sacred Light

Sheltered beneath the radiant beam,
We find our rest, like a gentle stream.
In the refuge of love so profound,
Peace envelops, in silence found.

Here, burdens lighten, sorrows cease,
In sacred light, we find release.
Every shadow is kissed by grace,
Illuminating our hidden space.

Voices uplifted in hymns of praise,
Hearts united in fervent gaze.
With each moment, faith entwines,
In the sanctuary, love defines.

Through trials faced, our spirits soar,
In the embrace of guidance, we explore.
Here, hope blossoms, like spring's first bloom,
Absorbing light, dispelling gloom.

Together we dwell in a sea of light,
Finding comfort in the sacred sight.
For in this haven, we truly belong,
The refuge of faith, where we grow strong.

From Darkness, the Light of Faith

In the depths where shadows cling tight,
We search for the spark, the glimmer of light.
In the struggle, our hearts unfold,
Rooted in hope, and stories told.

With whispers of courage, we stand tall,
Embracing the journey, answering the call.
For in the alleys where darkness does creep,
The light of faith awakens from sleep.

Each step in the silence, a beacon so bright,
Guiding the weary through the long night.
In unity forged by hands held high,
We rise together, our spirits comply.

Braving the storms, hearts intertwined,
Trusting the path that is clearly aligned.
With visions that promise to shatter the night,
We gather the strength, igniting our light.

So let us remember, in shadows we dwell,
The light of faith rings a beautiful bell.
It calls to the brave, the weary, the meek,
From darkness, we rise, and together we seek.

From Ashes to Grace

In shadows deep, we roam alone,
Yet faith is a seed, in hearts it's sown.
From ashes cold, we rise anew,
Embraced by love, our spirits true.

With every dawn, His mercy flows,
A gentle whisper in our throes.
Restoration found in His warm light,
From darkest hours to hopeful sight.

Each burden borne, a chance to heal,
In wounds we bear, His grace reveals.
Transcending pain, we learn to rise,
From grief to joy, beneath the skies.

In trials faced, His strength we gain,
Through storms of life, we break the chain.
From ashes cold, our hearts ignite,
With faith as flame, we claim our light.

Echoes of the Divine Flame

In silence deep, His voice we hear,
A whisper soft, dispelling fear.
Echoes of love, from heavens high,
Bathe us in grace, as stars pass by.

The flame within, forever bright,
Guides wanderers through the night.
With every heartbeat, we feel His grace,
In cherished moments, we find our place.

Through trials faced, His light remains,
In every sorrow, love sustains.
Embers of hope, forever aglow,
In the darkest times, He makes us grow.

Together we stand, hand in hand,
United in faith, a sacred band.
In sacred fires, our spirits soar,
Awakened to love, forevermore.

Embracing the Hidden Light

Within the soul, a treasure lies,
A hidden spark, beneath the skies.
In gentle whispers, truth takes flight,
Embracing the love, the hidden light.

Through valleys low and mountains steep,
His promise keeps, our hearts from sleep.
In each embrace, we find our way,
Guided by light, to brighter day.

With open hearts, we seek to find,
The beauty of love, the ties that bind.
In every trial, we rise and stand,
Embracing grace, hand in hand.

Let not the darkness steal our sight,
For even shadows yield to light.
With every breath, we choose to see,
The hidden love that sets us free.

The Silent Call of Hope

In quiet moments, hope awakens,
A melody sweet, softly taken.
With every sigh, the heart does yearn,
For love's embrace, a steady return.

The silence speaks, though words are few,
In gentle grace, He carries through.
Those weary souls who seek the dawn,
In darkest nights, hope lingers on.

Each tear that falls, a seed of change,
Transforming hearts, through love we range.
A silent call, a beacon bright,
Guiding the lost to find the light.

With every struggle, we stand tall,
Responding to that sacred call.
In faith we trust, in love we cope,
For in our hearts, resides pure hope.

Grace Descending Along Paths

In whispered prayers, we tread so light,
Each step a blessing, in day and night.
With souls uplifted, we seek the way,
Grace descending, shadows drift away.

In every heart, divine light glows bright,
A loving hand holds us through the fight.
With open arms, the heavens extend,
Guiding each soul, our spirits ascend.

Through trials faced, faith's embers ignite,
We rise in hope, through storm and plight.
Every burdened heart learns to trust,
In grace's embrace, a sacred must.

With gentle whispers, the angels sing,
A symphony of love that takes wing.
As we walk forward, hearts intertwined,
Grace leads the way, in peace we find.

So let us gather, in sacred space,
With open hearts, we feel His grace.
In every moment, we are made whole,
As grace descends, it blesses the soul.

The Phoenix of the Soul

From ashes deep, a spirit takes flight,
A sacred fire ignites the night.
With wings of hope, it soars above,
The Phoenix reborn, in radiant love.

In cycles of loss, we learn to grow,
Through pain and sorrow, the heart shall glow.
With every trial, a lesson we find,
The Phoenix awakens, the soul aligned.

In stillness we gather, beneath the stars,
Healing our wounds, though life leaves scars.
With courage wrapped in flames so bright,
The spirit rises, embracing the light.

In moments of doubt, hold on, endure,
Transformation awaits, of this be sure.
As embers fade, new dreams will unfold,
The Phoenix of the soul, a heart of gold.

With every dusk, a dawn shall appear,
The beauty of rebirth draws us near.
In unity, we find the strength to rise,
A journey eternal, in love's skies.

Softening the Hard Edges

In gentle waters, we learn to flow,
Softening hearts where love might grow.
With tender grace, each moment we mend,
Awakening light, where shadows descend.

Through trials faced, our spirits may bend,
But in the stillness, our hearts transcend.
With every tear, like rain from above,
We find the courage to blossom in love.

In nature's arms, we find our peace,
Whispers of wisdom, our fears release.
As petals unfold, unearthing the soul,
Softening edges, making us whole.

With open hands, we share our light,
In kindness wrapped, our souls take flight.
Together we journey, hand in hand,
Softening hearts across this land.

So let us gather, in warmth and embrace,
With gentle words, and a loving grace.
In every moment, let love be our guide,
Softening edges, with hope beside.

Revelations of the Silent Dawn

In quiet stillness, the dawn shall break,
Whispers of truth through shadows awake.
With each new ray, our hearts align,
Revelations heard, as stars resign.

In morning's grace, the world stands still,
As silence speaks, our souls it will.
With every breath, the spirit reveals,
The sacred secrets that love conceals.

Through fog and mist, the light draws near,
An unveiling journey, shedding fear.
With open eyes, we witness the glow,
In revelations where love can flow.

As day unfolds, we rise anew,
A promise kept in the morning's hue.
With hearts receptive, we journey on,
In the silent dawn, our fears are gone.

So let us gather, with hope in our hearts,
Embracing the light as the new day starts.
In every sunrise, divine whispers call,
Revelations of love that unite us all.

The Sacred Spear of Light

In the dawn where shadows flee,
A spear of light shines bright and free.
Guiding souls from dark despair,
It whispers hope into the air.

With each thrust through night's embrace,
It carves anew the sacred space.
Hearts awaken to the call,
United we shall stand, not fall.

Through valleys low and mountains high,
The sacred path we shall not shy.
As angels sing and spirits soar,
We march together evermore.

In silence found beneath the tree,
The sacred spear reveals to me.
The truth that blooms within our strife,
A testament to sacred life.

Embrace the light, cast off the night,
In unity, we find our might.
With faith our guide, we pierce the dark,
Forever blessed, we leave our mark.

Among the Holy Flames

Within the hearth where courage glows,
Among the flames, the spirit knows.
Each flicker speaks of love divine,
A warmth that binds our hearts in line.

In sacred dance, the embers rise,
They whisper truths to open skies.
Resilient faith ignites our soul,
As we give thanks, we feel made whole.

The holy flames consume our fears,
Through trials faced, we shed our tears.
In sacred circles, hand in hand,
We forge a bond few understand.

Each breath a prayer, each heartbeat song,
In unity, we all belong.
Among these flames our spirits soar,
Together stronger than before.

As day turns night, through ages passed,
The holy flames shall everlast.
With hearts ignited, we shall stand,
Together in this sacred land.

The Blessed Reawakening

In silence deep, the gardens bloom,
A blessed dawn dispels the gloom.
From slumber vast, our spirits rise,
To greet the light with open eyes.

A whisper sweeps through verdant leaves,
A call for all who seek and believe.
The truth within begins to shine,
As hearts unite in love divine.

Through trials faced, we find our way,
In each new dawn, in every day.
The blessed reawakening sings,
A promise held on angel's wings.

With every step, we shed the chains,
Embracing purpose in our pains.
The light ignites the path we tread,
As hope and faith become our bread.

Reborn anew, we rise and stand,
Together as one, hand in hand.
In this awakening, pure and bright,
We walk forever in the light.

Journey to the Infinite Horizon

On winds of faith, our spirits fly,
A journey set beneath the sky.
Towards horizons, vast and wide,
With love and hope, we shall abide.

Through valleys deep and mountains bold,
The story of our lives unfolds.
Each step we take, a dance of grace,
A sacred quest we all embrace.

In twilight's glow, we bind our dreams,
With unity, we weave our seams.
The stars our guide, the moon our light,
We venture forth into the night.

With open hearts and willing hands,
We journey forth across these lands.
In every heartbeat, joy aligns,
The infinite awaits, it shines.

Through trials faced and lessons learned,
Our spirits rise, our passions burned.
Together strong, we claim our place,
In journeys vast, we find our grace.

In the Garden of Hope

In the silence of morning, hope sings,
Where petals of promise gently sway.
Each blossom whispers of heavenly things,
In the arms of the light, we find our way.

Beneath the sky's vast, eternal dome,
Roots dig deep, drawing strength from the earth.
In this sacred space, we choose to roam,
Nourished by faith, we witness rebirth.

With every step, our burdens feel less,
The fragrance of grace fills the air so sweet.
In the garden of wisdom, we find our rest,
As the heart learns to dance to love's gentle beat.

Voices of angels in chorus reside,
Guiding us gently through trials and tears.
In the garden of solace, we abide,
Embraced by compassion, calming our fears.

Hope blooms eternal, in shadows and light,
A tapestry woven by hands of the divine.
In every moment, we gather our sight,
In the garden of hope, our spirits align.

Mending the Fragments in Light

In the tapestry of life, threads have frayed,
But love's gentle hand begins to weave.
Each shattered piece, in the sun's warm shade,
Mending the heart, teaching us to believe.

With every dawn, soft glimmers arise,
Shadows retreat, unveiling the day.
In the gaze of grace, we find our size,
Building foundations from what went astray.

Embracing the scars that tell our tale,
In the light of forgiveness, we stand tall.
Together we rise, through tempests we sail,
In the mending of fragments, we answer the call.

Whispers of mercy flow through the sky,
Binding our souls with threads of pure gold.
Though we may falter, we reach for the high,
In unity's strength, the new life unfolds.

The light that surrounds us is more than bright,
It's a promise kept through trials and strife.
In this sacred glow, we shine with delight,
Mending the fragments, we discover new life.

Cracks in the Darkness, Light Forth

In the shadows where sorrow holds sway,
A flicker of hope begins to ignite.
For every wound, there is a way,
To transform the despair into radiant light.

These cracks in the darkness are windows to grace,
Where the soul's quiet whispers start to arise.
In the stillness we find our rightful place,
And the burdens we carry turn into the skies.

With every tear, a river flows strong,
Carving our path through the roughest terrain.
From pain, we learn the depth of our song,
In the light's embrace, we find our refrain.

Through the cracks, a promise shines ever clear,
That love conquers all and binds us as one.
In the darkest of moments, we draw near,
Knowing the battle is already won.

So let light forth from the scars that we bear,
Transforming our stories into tales of grace.
Together we rise, through each whispered prayer,
Cracks in the darkness become love's embrace.

The Transformative Lament

In the stillness of night, hearts cry aloud,
A lament that echoes through valleys of pain.
Yet in every tear, we are nature's proud,
Finding strength in the sorrow, growth in the grain.

The weight of our burdens can shatter the soul,
But in surrender, we open the door.
From anguish, we learn that we are made whole,
In the transformative lament, we explore.

Here in the darkness, the spirit takes flight,
Wings formed from ashes, ready to rise.
With every lament, we embrace our own light,
Through the depths of despair, we find the skies.

Our voices entwined in a symphony deep,
Transforming our anguish to melodies sweet.
In vulnerability, promises we keep,
Singing through sorrow, our hearts skip a beat.

So let the lament be a pathway to peace,
A journey of grace that leads back to love.
With each heartfelt cry, the burdens release,
In the transformative lament, we rise above.

A Tapestry Woven in Faith

With threads of hope, we intertwine,
In every heart, His love will shine.
Each strand a prayer, each knot a grace,
Together we stand, in His embrace.

Through trials faced and storms we weather,
In unity, we rise together.
The weaving strong, the pattern clear,
In faith we find our path sincere.

The colors bright, in sorrow's night,
A tapestry of sacred light.
With every stitch, a story told,
In faith, our hearts are made of gold.

The fabric soft, yet woven tough,
A shield of love when times get rough.
In every tear, a joy reclaims,
In faith, we find our truest names.

Let not despair unbind our thread,
For in His arms, we are not dead.
With every dawn, a new design,
In faith, the world is truly mine.

The Light's Unyielding Embrace

In shadows deep, where doubts arise,
The light shines forth, a sweet surprise.
Its warmth envelops, dispels the cold,
A promise kept, a love retold.

Through whispered prayers and gentle tears,
The light of faith calms all our fears.
It guides our steps along the way,
The unyielding light of every day.

With every flicker, hope ignites,
In darkest hours, it brings the heights.
A beacon bright when troubles near,
In light, we trust, in light, we cheer.

Embrace the glow, let spirits soar,
In the light, we are evermore.
With open hearts, we boldly claim,
The sacred love that knows no shame.

As day turns to night, still we seek,
The light of grace, it makes us speak.
From within us, its presence burns,
In every soul, the light returns.

From Hollow Souls to Glimmering Hopes

In weary hearts, where shadows loom,
We find the space for grace to bloom.
From hollow cries and whispered fears,
To glimmering hopes that dry our tears.

Each step we take, a journey wide,
In faith we walk, with Him beside.
Through valleys low and mountains high,
Our souls take flight, on wings they fly.

With every dawn, new strength appears,
Transforming pain into our cheers.
From brokenness to vibrant dreams,
In faith, we mend all fractured seams.

The light that shines, a guiding trace,
Transforms our lives with boundless grace.
From shadows' grip, we now emerge,
In hope, our hearts begin to surge.

With every tear, a blessing born,
From hollow souls, new life is sworn.
Embrace the journey, trust the way,
In faith, we find a brighter day.

Echoes of Faith Beyond Darkness

In darkened rooms where silence reigns,
The echoes of faith break all the chains.
Whispers of hope through the night flow,
In the stillness, His mercy glows.

The spirit sings, though shadows fall,
In faith, we rise, we hear the call.
Beyond despair, our voices rise,
In echoes heard across the skies.

From deep within, our hearts ignite,
Turning darkness into brilliant light.
With every breath, a prayer we weave,
In faith's embrace, we will believe.

Through trials faced, we learn to see,
The path of love that sets us free.
Echoes of faith, a sweet refrain,
In victory, we'll break the chain.

No fear can hold us, no doubt can bind,
In faith united, our souls aligned.
With every echo, truth shall rise,
Beyond the dark, we claim the skies.

A Hymn of New Beginnings

In dawn's soft light we rise anew,
With faith embraced, our hearts are true.
Each breath a vow, each step a prayer,
In grace we find the courage there.

The past released, like autumn leaves,
In hope we plant what the Spirit weaves.
With every trial, we grow more strong,
The journey's path, where we belong.

The whispers of the divine ignite,
Guiding our souls through darkest night.
Together we sing in joyous refrain,
For blessings flow like gentle rain.

Our hearts aligned, as one we stand,
Embracing life with open hands.
In unity, our spirits soar,
To heights unknown, we seek to explore.

With every dawn, a chance to be,
The light within, our sacred plea.
A hymn of new begins today,
In love and light, we find our way.

Transcendence through Trials

In shadows deep, the Spirit calls,
With whispered strength, it never falls.
We rise through pain, like phoenix flight,
Transforming darkness into light.

Each burden borne, a lesson learned,
Through weary nights, our hearts have yearned.
In faith we tread the rugged way,
Emerging bright, we greet the day.

With every tear, a river flows,
Through trials faced, our spirit grows.
From ashes, we craft a vibrant song,
United in the hope we've long.

The path may twist, but we will find,
In struggle's grip, our hearts aligned.
Together we rise, forever free,
In transcendence, we seek to be.

So let us praise the strength within,
Through trials faced, we shall begin.
With every step, our spirits cheer,
In love unbound, we persevere.

The Sacred Ascent of Spirit

Upon the hill where visions dwell,
We climb in silence, hearts compel.
The air is thick with sacred grace,
In stillness found, we seek that place.

Each step a prayer, we rise above,
In unity, we share our love.
The light advances, our souls embrace,
Atop the world, in sacred space.

With every breath, the heavens speak,
In harmony, we find the peak.
Our hearts alight with visions clear,
In sacred ascent, we persevere.

The trials faced, now gently fade,
In this ascent, we are remade.
The Spirit dances, pure delight,
In shared ascent, we claim the bright.

So let the journey lift us high,
In unity, our spirits fly.
With joy we seek the sacred race,
Embraced by love in holy space.

Renewal in the Sacred Grove

In whispered winds, the ancient trees,
Invite our souls to find their ease.
In sacred groves, we seek to heal,
Transcending pain, our spirits feel.

With open hearts, we breathe the peace,
In nature's arms, our worries cease.
The gentle rustle, a hymn divine,
In every leaf, the light will shine.

Through roots that dig in sacred earth,
We find the essence of new birth.
A cycle turns, as seasons blend,
In nature’s heart, the soul ascends.

The sun will rise, the moon will wane,
In timeless dance, we greet the gain.
With every heartbeat, love will flow,
In sacred grove, we come to know.

So let us gather, hand in hand,
In sacred space, where spirits stand.
With gratitude we raise our voice,
In renewal's song, we find our choice.

From Despair to Divine Light

In shadows deep, the heart does ache,
A whisper soft, the soul's awake.
Through trials grim, a spark ignites,
From despair's grasp, we seek the light.

With faith as guide, we rise once more,
Each step we take, we start to soar.
In prayer's embrace, our fears take flight,
New dawn arises, dispelling night.

The heavens part, a voice so pure,
In love's sweet grace, our hearts endure.
Transformation blooms, from pain to peace,
In sacred trust, our burdens cease.

Through darkest hours, the spirit calls,
A promise bright, beyond these walls.
In unity, we find our way,
To sacred shores, where hope holds sway.

Together we walk, through fire and rain,
With every tear, we break the chain.
From despair's depths, the soul takes flight,
In joy's embrace, we find the light.

Beneath the Cloak of Suffering

Beneath the cloak of heavy grief,
We search for solace, yearn for relief.
In silence deep, our spirits cry,
Yet in our hearts, hope will not die.

Though shadows loom and paths are steep,
In every wound, a promise we keep.
Beneath the weight of sorrow's hold,
Lies the strength to rise, to be bold.

With hands uplifted, we seek the grace,
That shines through trials, in every place.
Each prayer ascends, a fragrant plea,
In suffering's grip, we're set free.

The light of faith, a beacon bright,
Guides us onward, ignites the night.
Through pain and loss, the soul grows wise,
In every tear, a chance to rise.

So let us walk, though weary still,
With hearts entwined, we bend our will.
Beneath the cloak, we find our strength,
In love's embrace, we go to great lengths.

Serenity’s Triumph over Darkness

When chaos reigns, and shadows spread,
In stillness found, our hearts are led.
To waters calm, where peace resides,
In quiet moments, the soul abides.

Through trials storm, we learn to breathe,
In faith's warm glow, our fears we leave.
With every storm that passes by,
We rise in grace, our spirits high.

The dawn will break, with gentle light,
Awakening dreams from long, deep night.
With hearts aligned to love's pure tune,
We find our path beneath the moon.

Embrace the calm, let go of strife,
In serenity, we uncover life.
With open hands, we share our grace,
In love's warm light, we find our place.

Together we stand, in joy and peace,
In unity's bond, our fears release.
Through light and shade, our spirits soar,
In tranquil hearts, we seek for more.

The Path of Spiritual Resurrection

On paths unknown, where shadows weave,
With faith as fire, we learn to believe.
From ashes rise, the spirit renewed,
In sacred moments, we are imbued.

Each step we take, transformation's grace,
A journey deep, in time and space.
Through trials faced, we shed the old,
In love's embrace, we are made bold.

The cross we bear, a weight we share,
In every burden, the hope laid bare.
With open hearts, we seek the dawn,
In gentle whispers, new lives are drawn.

In unity's bond, we find our way,
Through darkened nights, to brighter days.
With every breath, our spirits rise,
In resurrection, we claim the skies.

Let not the past hold back our flight,
For in each moment, we find our light.
With every dawn, the world reborn,
In love's pure truth, our hearts are sworn.

Glimmers Beyond the Veil

In shadows deep, the spirit yearns,
To catch a glimpse where the light returns.
Each whisper holds a sacred call,
A promise wrapped in the cosmic thrall.

Through trials faced and tears we shed,
A guiding star, where angels tread.
In quiet moments, faith ignites,
Hope rises high to embrace the lights.

Waves of grace, like morning dew,
Caress the heart and make it new.
In every prayer, a fertile ground,
In silence, sacred truths abound.

Veils may shimmer, yet love prevails,
Leading us through these winding trails.
Beyond the dark, a promise grand,
Eternal peace, a holy hand.

So, seek the glimmers, chase the light,
For heaven's glow will guide our flight.
With every breath, let spirits soar,
To realms unseen, forevermore.

Rebirth in Sacred Stone

From dust to dawn, the earth will sing,
Of stories lost and the life they bring.
In quiet chambers, the spirit stirs,
Embracing all that time endures.

Ancient whispers touch the soul,
As stones remember and make us whole.
Each crack a path to what has been,
A saga told in every sin.

With every heartbeat, echoes call,
A resurrection from the fall.
Through trials worn and shadows cast,
We find the strength to hold steadfast.

In sacred stones, the truth shall shine,
A mirrored dance of the divine.
With open hearts, we join the dance,
In every moment, find our chance.

Rebirth awaits, as night turns day,
In every prayer, we find our way.
Embrace the cycle, let life flow,
In sacred stone, our spirits grow.

The Journey into Radiance

Beneath the sky, the pathway glows,
With every step, the spirit knows.
Through valleys low and mountains high,
We journey forth, where eagles fly.

In solitude, the heart will gleam,
Awaking visions, like a dream.
Each moment brightens, revealing ways,
In love's embrace, the spirit sways.

The trials faced, like shadows cast,
Are lessons learned, a die is passed.
With courage found in depths of night,
The heart shall guide us to the light.

Step by step, we cast the fears,
Through sacred waters, cleanse the tears.
In every heartbeat, love ignites,
We journey onward, towards the heights.

With arms outstretched and heart aglow,
We seek the truth only love can know.
The journey deep, the radiance near,
In fields of grace, we shed all fear.

Awakening the Inner Messiah

In silence dwells the holy spark,
A whisper loud within the dark.
With every breath, the truth awakes,
A journey deep that love partakes.

To rise above our worldly chains,
And search for peace beyond the pains.
With open hearts, we seek the flame,
Awakening God within our name.

In every soul, a light does shine,
A clear reflection of the divine.
Through joy and sorrow, we shall find,
The sacred dance of heart and mind.

Embrace the trial, embrace the grace,
For in our darkness, light finds place.
Each act of love, a burst of truth,
Awakens hope, renews our youth.

The inner messiah, strong and bright,
Illuminates our darkest night.
In unity, we rise above,
To share the glory, and spread the love.

Milton Keynes UK
Ingram Content Group UK Ltd.
UKHW020039271124
451585UK00012B/940

9 789916 898840